Ink

Poetry

By Vickie Johnstone

AF505130

Ink
A collection of 74 poems.
© Copyright May 18, 2023, Vickie Johnstone.
Published May 18, 2023 by Vickie Johnstone.
All poems, except *Judder*, written between April 2, 2022 and May 14, 2023.

© All rights reserved.

Draft2Digital Edition.

No part of this publication may be reproduced, stored in a retrieval system, or transmitted in any form or by any means without the prior permission in writing of the publisher, Vickie Johnstone, nor be circulated in any form of binding or cover other than that in which it is published.

Cover image: istockphoto/LuckyTD

Dedication

Dedicated to my grandparents,
three of whom left us far too soon
and one who lived a colourful life
until the grand old age of 101.
I treasure my memories of
you.

Books by the author

Tirips Shade
3 Heads & a Tail

Cerulean Songs
The Sea Inside (book 1)

I Dream of Zombies
I Dream of Zombies (book 1)
Haven (book 2)

The Kiwi Series
Kiwi in Cat City (book 1)
Kiwi and the Missing Magic (book 2)
Kiwi and the Living Nightmare (book 3)
Kiwi and the Serpent of the Isle (book 4)
Kiwi in the Realm of Ra (book 5)
Kiwi's Christmas Tail (book 6)

Smarts & Dewdrop Series
Day of the Living Pizza (book 1)
Day of the Pesky Shadow (book 2)

Poetry
Kaleidoscope
Life's Rhythms (haiku)
Travelling Light
Mind-spinning Rainbows
A Poem a Day
Between the Sky and the Sea
Ink
Woman
Meditations (haiku)

Others
The Gage Project
Stand Together: A Collection of Poems and Short Stories for Ukraine
A Very Zombie Christmas

Poems

Crossing water
The hotel room
Season's tunes
Daily bread
Out
Silver
Five answers to the same question
Spring awakes with daffodils
Jackdaw
In the backyard
The same time
White light
The four-pronged fork
The bracelet
With time
The circle
It's time for walkies
Prisoners of war
Balls
A bird in the hand
The meadow
Tails
Worms
Lost & Found
Gold
Superstition
Hourglass
The alter ego (gecko)

Ink

We are ink,
dotted on paper,
mute words waiting
for a voice to awaken them,
inquisitive hands to turn the pages,
open eyes to read the hidden,
empathy to wish to know,
pour out its warmth,
and be.

May 14, 2023

The surging sea

It's something beyond words,
this speaking without saying anything at all,
none of the creations inside your head,
an outer world of living inner space,
this seeing without seeing,
a pull beyond the other world.

And here we pause before the rosebud sea,
this sheer wild energy, a surging out
of truth, ideas and pure patience.
Feel lost in the rush of it, the subtle shift,
the stifled air purified with salt,
the knowing without a reason to know.

It bends and rides and finds us here,
travels straight through us,
beyond the day and over the night,
and we can bear it, full-on, full force,
for we are with it, in it, of it,
and all the rest is white, white noise.

May 8-9, 2023

Dedicated to my mum. Inspired by a story she once told me.

Wild horses

She sees horses in the streets,
tearing down the tarmac,
silvery manes of flowing water
twisting in the wind's hands.

Pale white streaks of ghosts
leaving translucent trails of light,
black eyes glistening, nostrils
flared, silent in their insistency.

They say the fields are full of
bodies, buried during the war,
but all she can see are the horses,
hooves pounding the ground.

Beautiful wild beasts racing
without a care in the world,
unreflected in windows.
How they run.

August 18, 2022

Betrayal

Betrayal, cuts like ice.
Tanglewood and barbed thorns,
existential murmurs of doubt.
An open wound, etched deep,
it sucks time into itself,
lingers, leaves a white trail of scar,
translucent tissue in the light.

You can feel it at your back,
a heaviness, a sack of empty.
It follows you as you cross the street,
as you enter a building,
as you try to eat, try to swallow.
It sits like coal in the pit of your being,
seeking to consume you whole.

You look at the scar sometimes.
It represents a turning, a dark page,
an entry point into the netherworld,
where Persephone sits and contemplates
the springtime light of the world above.
Sometimes the scar stares back,
a reminder of who you were,
and who you are, written in water.

May 11, 2023

Ring the alarm

Flag that car for a lift,
and you might not get very far.

Walk the streets late at night,
be careful where you are.

Ride a bike, so then drive slow,
or you might not make it home.

Fly a plane, check the seat,
be sure to sit right by the exit.

Stay in a hotel, look at the number,
ensure it doesn't say thirteen.

Buy a lock, buy an alarm, buy a dog,
buy a gun, buy a knife, learn to run,
learn to fight, check for streetlights,
check behind you, check in front.

Don't get the nightbus,
do get the nightbus.

Don't walk,
walk.

Don't, don't, don't...

Just stay home.

March 25, 2023

Boxes

The man with the can with the water
says you need to stay put where you are,
you can't spread out your roots any further.
Keep your unruly branches straight as a die,
open your leaves, but only so far – don't overstep,
whatever you do, don't overshadow the other plants.
Stay in your box, even if you can't breathe.
The air you've been given should always suffice.

If you need inspiration, gaze straight up.
The sky's the limit, but it's way out of reach.
This yellow sun will ensure your leaves grow,
this blue dew will saturate in the pink-eyed dawn,
so try to catch as much as you can in your hands.
He'll follow it up, the man with the can,
when he comes to your neighbourhood.
He might even splurge you some *Baby Bio*.

Stretch your woody limbs high when the sun shines,
furl your leaves and creep on down in a tumult of rain,
unless you love to dance inside those silver showers,
and then be my guest, so long as no one else sees,
or they might think you're trying to attract attention,
and you need to stay in your box. Keep quiet.

In order to grow, you have to stay where you are.
We need to know where you are. You're on our list of
faceless millions. No name. Just a number. That's all we need.
So don't shine. Come rain or fine we'll know you're here,
quietly swaying in your bright red box, leaves pruned,
stretching your limbs towards a sun you can't reach.

February 28, 2023

Shatter

We are but the darkest glass,
prisms turning, starkest shine,
and here in glass we reside.

We taste the bitter-sweetest salt
of the surging rush of sea below
and cloak ourselves in the cyan eyes
of the stillest tranquil sky above,
view laughing dolphins arching loops
over these aching oceans deep
with scarlet love, and we ourselves
are but glass, cut-outs spilling ideas,
a realm of secret colour undefined,
steadfast, yet ever breakable,
our fragility misting our acumen.

Stones could shatter us,
and yet we dwell beside them,
knowing how brittle are our bones.

The collector gathers memories,
new and old, spectres breathing in grey,
mirrors of all the things we have lived,
all the facets that make us human,
our passions, our guileless empathy,
all so steeped in hue, in so fragile words,
and yet we can never be forsaken
to one another. For we are, in our minds,
as we are, purest glass.

April 29, 2023

Binary

Binary, an adjective
made up of two things, two parts,
relating to, or belonging to a system
numerical, an umbilical cord
between numbers. A system with two
as its base, a pair – not one,
not alone.

There are two possible values here,
only two, no more, no more complex
than a couple, the ideal, the constant
companion, the support network we crave.
This bit, this binary digit, this open hand
of data, shedding light in a complex
universe.

When binary is fleshed out, a fingerprint,
emits a heartbeat, it's a system of two genders,
male and female, assigned at birth.
But we can go further now than binary,
into non-binary, gender fluid, a glide
between the two, an identity neither male
nor female.

It is only you. We are not the same.
We are not data. We are individual.
And we are not alone.

April 11, 2023

Spiral

To the in-between,
red spiral walking,
an unravelling ribbon
like the bent stem of a flower,
clipped wing of a bird,
cry of a raven.

It all sleeps, dwells, echoes,
filling and un-filling.

We are the awake,
biding our flimsy time,
listening to nature open
while welcoming the dawn in,
this pink rising splendour,
awaiting a spillage of yolk.

May 13, 2023

Mobiles & mosaics

In the middle of the boneyard,
cross-legged like a Buddha,
he sits amidst his art –
yesterday's throwaways,
a cavalcade of lived rubbish,
myriad lost colours and fabrics,
metals, paper, sticks and yarn.

He recreates the world in miniature,
idly watching his garden grow
from disfunction into movement,
hazy flowers from tight bulbs,
sprouting into perfume around him.
It makes him proud, the shapes
he sculpts with his gnarled hands.

The lightest touch, secret
caresses on the wind. Mosaics
witness nature's cracks reformed,
mirrors blotched, sound sprinkling
from a mobile spinning around
and around, echoing, re-evaluating,
rebecoming something new.

August 1, 2022

This poem was written from a prompt on NaPoWriMo.net: find a poem and write a new poem with the shape of the original in which every line starts with the first letter of the corresponding line in the original. I chose 'Ariel' by Sylvia Plath. This poem follows the initial letters, structure, syllables and word count.

Film reel

Seeking lost pleasures,
teased out of our spent time,
pursed be our lips, speechless.

Go find greatness,
happy as we sow,
pining for its might! – This fortune

slows to a film reel, bends to
time's slight touch,
of being and living in light.

Now stolen,
burial brings
honour –

books and dreams are
shimmerings.
Stolen ideas

hail from somewhere –
thoughts flown;
fluid walks a life.

Weary
gods, they listen –
dark karma will guide you.

A moment stops,
frozen, an empty course of water.
The still pause

makes all things melt.
And time,
a simple thread.

This is the new,
sewn into the sun-struck morning,
into the blue,

Everyman waking, reliving it all.

April 7, 2022

Bark whisperings

Whisperings of bark cracking,   pink streaks   of light writing words   in arching skies,
cradled in cloud hands.   Dew glistens on veined leaves,   their sides curling up
into a beating heart,   nature's prize.   Listen to the budding breath,   the distant sigh of
the undergrowth,   roots spreading out beneath the earth   carrying currents between
the trees,   an underground network of truth,   communicating through moss.

This green, lush land   aches with the weight of eras,   speaks its histories   in accents
we can't understand,   but we can place an ear   to the peeling bark   and contemplate.

An experiment in Kew   lets you hear   the pop,   the hiss,   the click-clack
of sap   streaking through the vessels   of saplings,   from the trunk up to   the leaves
swishing in the breeze.   Hear the heart of nature   pumping   from the inside,
transpiration and exhilaration   a chase of water,   the lifeblood of the trees,
and wait   for the blackbirds to land,   cosy down into their   twig nests   on high.

In the dawn chorus   you'll hear them sing   of their ancestors,   a mist of melodies
echoing from the treetops,   songs leaking   through the skies   to wake the morning.

And we'll chase life   through the deep, damp woods,   ground squelching   beneath us,
leading us in,   into the recesses,   light streaking the ground   from above
into the verdancy,   into the hidden places,   into the dark   where the earth smells green.

March 18, 2023

Straight

From the hip-hop bars
to the reggae stars
to the metal allegiance,
they're giving it one love,
showing the proof,
'ain't that the truth,
of how things can be,
the constant tree.

From small acorns...
and the spirit yearns.

From division to separation
to letting things see,
unity out of segregation,
bringing it in, no fee,
undivided, unseparated,
we count the names narrated.
The newborn cries an untold story,
the old looks back in memory.

Flick forward,
flick back.

The jumping jack grinning
as the world keeps spinning
on its wheels,
hoping everyone heals.
You wanna jump from the sky
cos it's oh so high,
but you're no longer falling,
where you came a-crawling,

seeing what's right,
keeping in the light.

July 26, 2022

The rush

There's a guitar solo
whipping through the crowd,
and a drum roll
as a zillion heads are bobbing
like an endless sea of hair.

The lead man's singing
in his denim, big boots,
leather waistcoat open,
microphone gripped like a lolly-pop.

I can't fathom what he's singing,
but I know it's gotta be good.

I'm so far back
he could be talking French,
but there's a rush in the air,
an electricity,
and it's building,
building...

everyone can feel it,
this gathering of sound;
the bass guitarist
is taking centre-stage,
snaking,
and he's on fire.

April 14, 2022

Webs

Accusations fly. Someone reads down the minutes
of the meeting. Stories grow leaves, seeds sown.
Is anyone asking if they are true? The spider
weaves its sticky web and words walk.
Years upon years upon years.

They gain courage backstage, spread thin
over the walls, into the cracks, seeping through.
Those on the stage go through the motions
as lines write themselves upon the floor.
Words spiral like smoke to fill the air.
Years upon years upon years.

Sentences come together in silence.
Outside, rain collects in the guttering.
It's a one-sided view down the avenue.

June 11, 2022

A different way of seeing

I see a world without guns,
without animosity or hate,
where kids can walk to school
and not be harmed by a stranger,
where a child won't be killed at home
by those meant to protect him.

There are no police sirens
flooding the spilt summer streets
because this world is devoid of violence.
Everyone inside is shielded from harm.

There are no knives being carried
in pockets out of fear of attack
or a desire to do harm to another.
There are no wars between nations
and murder is an uninvented word.
Segregation is unheard of.

There are no twists in the tale,
no desire to whip up hate,
no prejudices. There is only calm
in this new world, no bitter pill,
only joy and a happy spell
of the imagination.

June 6, 2022

Companions

Old Man Noble
with this ghost-string hair,
watches from the stables
where the horses gather him
in like family. He smells
of their hide, shares the same
black eyes, the steely stare.

He watches the moon dance in,
star stragglers in her wake.
All is silence while he hums
the memory of his yesterdays,
turning driftwood into gold.
These days are charmed for him,
not steeling the warmth within.

In the stables the mares nod,
sigh and shuffle beside him.
They lay down as he sleeps,
sharing their body heat.
And in the Dreaming time,
he listens to the chicken
bones sing.

September 4, 2022

Echoes

A mound of words
lost in a white shag-pile carpet.

A woman runs barefoot through the cool surf
bubbling on the edge of a pristine beach,
toes sinking in. Her prints echo in the sand,
a route for others to follow.

Grey gulls twist,
sailing on the backdraft,
voices transported on the wind.

The ringbearer scales the mountain,
where wild goats clamber on the diagonal,
mounting invisible steps with ease.

A world of opportunity waits below the sun,
its environs inconducive to man.

The man peddling just keeps going,
watching a faraway scene on a video screen.

March 20, 2023

This poem was written from a prompt on NaPoWriMo.net.
Prompt: write a poem that contains at least one of a different kind of simile – an epic simile. These are
basically extended similes that develop over multiple lines.

Flash of orange

As the train trundled out of the grey station,
the eager man in his orange, reflective vest
blazed his way through the carriage
like an orangutan swinging between branches,
looking for the swiftest route through
the fervent foliage and busyness of leaves.

He grasped each metal pole as if it were
a leafy rope of green, bristling with burs,
dangling from the gasping trees of the
languid rainforest, his skin sweating profusely
in the sauna-like heat of the black tunnel.

The other passengers veered backwards,
into the recesses, not wanting to make contact
or slow him down, so candidly intent was his
expression on becoming the king of this
urban metal-can jungle.

April 26, 2022

Seconds

The forgetting time ticks.
It doesn't have a hall pass,
or a bell to herald its arrival.
In it walks with a sashay,
pendulum slashing the air,
silver lace filigree hung free.
Softly serenade the seconds,
the choke of the hour loud.
And in the moment changed
we invent the forgetting time.

June 14, 2022

Just read about the coming vote on the Hunting Trophies (Import Prohibition) Bill. Sir Ranulph Fiennes is quoted as saying: "British trophy hunters are killing lions that have been snatched from their mothers & reared as pets. They are then shot in enclosures." If passed, the Bill will prohibit the import of endangered species as hunting trophies into the UK, helping to reduce the threats these animals face. Over the last 50 years, global wildlife has declined by 60%. About 25,000 trophy animals have been brought into the UK since the 1980s. So I wrote a poem about it. Endangered species deserve a voice.

Trophy

He's dreaming of the things he should have had.
Freedom.
To think. To be. To roam.
Family.
Peace of mind.
Relative safety.

He would always have stood a chance.
He could always have made a getaway.

But they stole him from his mother
when he was too young to roar.
They took him home, pampered him,
treated him like one of the family,
this human replacement,
but their humanity was just an act.

The cage was built just for him.
It fitted his dimensions exactly.

In silence, he raged against the bars,
trod the edges back and forth,
shook his mane, muscles rippling.
Eyes watched him through the lines,
sized him up,
saw him as the enemy,
easy pickings.

His gut instinct told him
it was all wrong,
yet no one came to free him
until the final hour.

He could have outrun them,
but there was nowhere to run.

He might have beaten them
if the fight had been fair,
and they were all unarmed.
But it was weighted against him.

Cornered.
Shot.
Dead.

His head is on their wall,
above a wooden mantelpiece
filled with family photographs.
Below, there's a gathering with wine.
They forgot to toast him,
too busy planning their next kill.

March 16, 2023

This poem was written from a prompt on NaPoWriMo.net.
Prompt: go to a book you love. Find a short line that strikes you. Make that line the title of your poem.
Write a poem inspired by the line. I've chosen the first line of the poem 'After a long dry spell',
from 'The Half-Finished Heaven' by Tomas Transtromer, whose poetry I love.

The summer is grey now strange evening

and daylight is a figment forgotten
as the land wrestles with the sky
for a spit of line so hard to define
we fail in dreaming of it. Distance
is a wild expanse of neverending time,
blown in on the tide, cast in and out,
an effervescent rush of hope. And now
we bend to the trees gaping at the wind,
rustling, whispering among the shadows,
making spectres thin, leaves whistling.
The air carries the subtle scent of green,
speckles of the early evening rain hang,
bubbles of light drawn in upon silence,
impenetrable, believing in the morrow.

May 12, 2022

This poem was written from a prompt on NaPoWriMo.net.
Prompt: I'd like to challenge you to write a 'duplex', which is a variation on the sonnet, developed by the poet
Jericho Brown. Like a typical sonnet, a duplex has 14 lines. It is organized into seven two-line stanzas.
The second line of the first stanza is echoed by (but not identical to) the first line of the second stanza, the
second line of the second stanza is echoed by (but not identical to) the first line of the third stanza, and so on.
The last line of the poem is the same as the first.

Invasion

You can feel the chill of death divide the sky.
From dawn til dusk the cruel torrent falls.

There is never a pause from dawn til dusk,
as we listen for the siren call to pierce the quiet.

The sirens and the bombs pierce the night,
down to the metro, where we hide our heads.

We hide our heads hoping for a new tomorrow,
but this has been our dismal fate for months.

This cannot be our fate, to have to suffer like this;
we are bombarded, tortured and intimidated,

but still we stand, bombarded, intimidated as we are.
Some of us have lost our fathers, our wives, our babes.

Only yesterday we embraced our fathers, wives, our babes.
You can feel the chill of death divide the sky.

April 27, 2022

This poem was written from a prompt on the NaPoWriMo website.
Prompt: sometimes writing poetry is a matter of getting outside of your own head and learning to see the world in a new way. To an extent, you have to 'derange' yourself – make the world strange and see it as a stranger might. To help you do that, I'd like to challenge you to write a poem inspired by this animated version of 'Seductive Fantasy' by Sun Ra and his Arkestra.

Planet pop

Coloured waves of sound
punctuate, take us on a trip,
blowing faint, blowing loud,
sound under sound, a sonophonic
breath. Spiral echoes of the same
float in and out on rolling surf
of plenitude. The planets swirl,
alien faces peek from clouds of pink
neon flutters. Leafy long plants pop
and grow, in rhythm, to be sucked
back into ground. It's a planet pop.
Red glow the fluorescent butterflies,
the Salvador Dali strokes of paint,
sliding and dripping picturesque.
The trumpet sounds its dreamscape,
outstretched hands hold life up.

May 2, 2022

Prompt: write a poem about a very small thing. Whether it's an atom, a button, a hummingbird's egg, dollhouse furniture or the mythical world's smallest violin, I hope you enjoy your poetic adventures into the microscopic.

All the small things

What is small?
The opposite of big.
The whimsical imaginable
enclosed in the miniscule.

A raindrop sliding off a petal
to take its final plunge into the void,
the fluff of a honey bee's bum
as it dives into a trumpet of pollen,
a pea as it pops its green pod,
the cry of a newborn kitten,
tiny flowers on a sunflower's head,
a leaf-cutter ant balancing his load.

A crumb,
a wisp of air,
a snapped twig,
an empty gesture,
a farewell lost on the wind,
flecks of sand blown on your cheek,
the salt of the sea tickling your lip,
a strand of silken hair.

But the very smallest thing
in this whole universe is a
quark. And it might be made of
nothing at all.

April 12, 2022

This poem was written from a prompt on NaPoWriMo.net.
Prompt: in honour of the potential luckiness of the number 13, I challenge you to write a poem that, like the
example poem, joyfully states that 'Everything is Going to Be Amazing'.

Under sun

Joy is a rosebud.
We are eager for it to open,
revealing its silken truth,
the pollen at its heart,
holding promise
like a rainbow.

April 13, 2022

I saw a man walking four dogs

The March air is damp with expectation.
You can smell the green, the woody bark,
the mix of flora, fumes and breath,
becoming headier before it arrives,
this drizzle, sliding down in a thin stream,
an invisible drummer on paving stones.

He walks four dogs, this wiry man,
back stooping, flat cap reflecting the rain.
Neatly, they walk in file behind him,
tails swaying to and fro to a distant beat,
paws padding in time, as though listening
to a doggy tune only they can hear.

Leather leads dangle, trail on the ground,
but the dogs don't try to drag them away.
There is no hurry here, no impatience.
It's a Sunday jaunt, a time-travel déjà vu –
they've done this walk day-in, day-out,
twice a day, three if they're in luck.

Come rain or come grey, snow or fine,
from house to park they walk this line
and back again, but it's never the same.
The dogs recognise some steps and voices,
can hear them coming around the block,
yet there's always something new.

The old man is silent, lost in a daydream
of the partner he used to share this with,
the route ingrained in his memory.
He loves the habit of it, the empathy.
From a distance they form a unit,
a furry, eighteen-legged family.

March 24, 2023

The storm

They counted names in the early hours
of the storm as the rain screeched down,
read them from the *Register*,
while someone twisted Rosary beads.
It ripped right through.

Mud flowed, slid and spilled,
overcame everything in its wake,
a 20 mile-per-hour gush
of boulders, debris, mud and branches.
Every building sank beneath the tonnage,
roofs and structures swept away,
photos depicting a lifetime.

They counted names,
but not all were accounted for.
They carved their names in wood,
so they would be remembered.
But we remembered them all.
Every single one.

March 2, 2023

This poem was written from a prompt on NaPoWriMo.net.
Prompt: this is a fun one – it's a prompt developed by the comic artist Lynda Barry, and it asks you to think about dogs you have known, seen or heard about, and use them as a springboard into wherever they take you.

Let's talk about dogs

Let's talk about dogs, baby,
what they mean to you and me –
to all the dogs we've ever known
and cherished down the road.

They bark a lot, as we know,
roll around in fox poo and dribble, oh,
eat you out of house and home,
and chew your favourite high heels,

But with a big, brown-eyed stare,
they've really got you there,
and you can't ever say no
to wherever they want to go.

You're sucker-punched,
and you know you're all theirs.
there's a lead on the back door
and it's time for walkies.

April 17, 2022

Drift

Driftwood,
the ebb and the flow and the flood,
where breath comes to stop and start,
and here we are, treading water,
adrift in the darkest ocean currents
tugging us outwards, every which way,
our lucid dreams, our raw necessities,
and how we would if we only could.

Driftwood,
how we see ourselves in our built reality,
requiring a map to find where we are,
the need to be and the need to be of,
and the constant doubt inside,
adapting to the push and pull of life,
this wash of minutes, hours, days,
the inability to press on Pause.

Driftwood,
where we meander in our wanderings,
our musings under a rain of trees,
their wild leaf hair trickling all around us,
like a verdant shield of purest light,
so we can try to live without thorns,
the constant rub of something wrong,
a hole in the heart of our being.

May 10, 2023

This poem was written from a prompt on NaPoWriMo.net.
Prompt: this prompt is based on Robert Hass's remarkable prose poem, 'A Story About the Body'. The idea is to write your own prose poem that is a story about the body.

A story about the body

One step forward, he stands alone, taking Sunday for granted, making it his own. One step back, he speaks alone, never takes people for granted, this rolling stone.

April 2, 2022

Wrapped

6 years old.
This gift is 6 years old.
Turn it over and the cover changes.
Twist it back, it's as it ever was.

A mirage of light,
without any shimmer.

There is an ink-black shadow within,
a portal to a place you won't want to know,
the hall of painted mirrors,
the expressive smokescreen,
the footprints trapped in snow.

It's a world of ice inside,
where you'll search for Mr Tumnus,
loiter beside the giant iron light,
waiting for the sun to thaw.

March 15, 2023

Grief

In spaces,
we tread spaces,
in circles winding,
forever spiralling,
this never ending,
this expanse of heart.
The emptying,
so severed links,
grey gusts twisting
from broken hands,
as we sink lower
into still blue water,
numbers marking how
out of depth we seem,
sliding in this endless
fade into the deep,
into the ever,
this dark arc rising
in silent speech
to greet us.

February 4, 2023

Starlings

His last words floated,
soared into a sky of curious birds,
murmurations of past lives twisting,
floating in the ether of yesterday,
the truancy of angels.

Friends wait in hesitation below,
unsure of raising a glass in respect,
unsure if it's the right thing to do,
stalling 'til the son takes the lead.

"It's a fine day for it," people said,
nodding knowingly, in that polite way,
too English to say how they feel,
keeping it in, stiff upper lip and all.

Everyone can feel the hole.
It spreads outwards in violet hush,
memories filling with postcards
of happy days and well-worn anecdotes,
offering a bright light in the cold.

Above, the starlings are spinning,
creating pictures in the quiet air,
filling their audience with hope,
honouring he who has passed.

February 11, 2023

Wildflowers of Solace

Dithering on maybe, we wish awhile, wonder
where the story leads us, wishing on a mile
of things yonder as the spiky trees grow wilder,
and plants thicker, the woolly undergrowth a mix
of wild things, pouting flowers, thistles, meandering
lines of minted leaves betwixt butterflies' wings
yawning wide, and the scent carries, inspiring bumble
bees, their sprightly buzz slipping in air like a light mower,
arcs of sunlight mosaic glinting on their gossamer wings,
this smooth lace, flickering, darting in and out of
pollen-filled horns, the gooey yellow thickness sticking
to their stripey bodies vibrating, hovering, dew delicately
balanced on all the edges, velveteen and surviving.

September 6, 2022

Fast-forward in slow

We come and go, ebb and flow,
wildest dreams and bygone years
remembered. Star bright and sky burn,
some lives lived too close to the sun.

We try not to lose our individuality,
collecting alternate patterns to stand out,
colours full-raze, imitating a craze,
and languid days we draw resplendent.

Here is truth in our hands, and we hold it
aloft, clear waters, reflecting our real selves.
We glance back from our fast-forward,
thankful to have known those we miss,

curious to know who has yet to arrive,
opening doors and closing the well-worn,
to bring us knowledge and fulfilment
on our journey to the edge of the world.

March 8, 2023

Snow road

What's it like to be followed,
live your life under the paparazzi,
have your every move read out loud,
portions embellished for amusement,
a coffee book of your inside self?
But you didn't give permission.

I see you looking for a way out,
but you'd need to walk back a decade
for the peace of mind you used to know,
the privacy, an anonymity of being.

You live inside this aperture, the
narrow space the camera lets you have –
in focus, out, it's all the same. The game
set up, already played, you find your space
on the board, every pawn assembled.
Snakes and Ladders has fairer rules.

You don't know how much time you have,
so you fill it with everyone you know.

There's a car stuck at the end of the road.
The driver sits, hidden by silver birch,
but you can sense him contemplating.
Beyond, the road breaks, runs out,
but the car blocks the view. Snow drifts.
Summer sells itself short. All things

shapeshift, blur out of focus. There's
just the road where things happen.
The day makes choices and clicks the
shutter back. A red deer is crossing.
Its black eyes mark the observer.
Caught in headlights, it won't move,
only linger, not knowing where to go.

June 19, 2022

Ashes

Where the tallest of the Ash trees walk,
they fill the translucent air with sighs,
gesticulating branches ever-twisting,
painting pictures in their wand'rings.

Giants, their stuck-up hair peeks on high,
emerald scraggly, shadowed by cloud.
Words are invisible childlike scrawls,
planted in the way seeds become ideas,
full-leafed, moisture-licked, all green,
sap sneaking from fine fissures.

Cutter ants heft their sea of prizes,
shimmer through on stick legs, troops
marching over all these exposed roots
until the tallest trees rise to take their walk
back into their viridescent treasured past,
all the ages covered, seen and unseen,
the trials and endeavours they have witnessed.
These rings within mark their truth.

February 24, 2023

Fluidity

It begins light,
flickers, so slight,
no sound, only specks,
colourless. Fuelled by
air, it gusts, stoked,
drums a rhythm on
car roofs, sweeps the
streets, circling drains.

It uproots, saturates,
a sound curve builds
into a haze of reckoning.
This sheet of water
cascades, envelops,
awakening everything.
New growth, fresh air.
The smell of green.

July 31, 2022

This poem was written from a prompt on NaPoWriMo.net.
Prompt: in honour of the always becoming nature of poetry, I challenge you to select a photograph from the perpetually disconcerting @SpaceLiminalBot and write a poem inspired by one of these odd, in-transition spaces.

Misted

Misted light,
a heart of deep blue.
Cars skate in white lace,
strewn across the ground
like rice, sinking in sound.
Windows stare out blankly,
silent and solemn from angular
walls, waiting for a semblance of
light. But there is just this half-glow,
a slight wink, this partial serenade
to the beckoning night. All things
must close. The firefly lights in the
rooms flicker off, one by one, until
only the blue survives.

May 5, 2022

Judder

Is this a rip in time
where we judder on repeat,
anchors set midway,
never up, never down?

We count stories backwards
instead of reading the lines,
watch birds walk on water
and whales mount the skies.

We float in discrete bubbles,
apart, not feeling true,
wrapped inside cotton clouds,
looking for a voice.

With the world we are done,
only waiting on the freeway
while neon signs on-off wink
to a twisted track of sunlight

carried in on the ebb and flow.
Drill your toes into wet sand,
and feel the sun creep inside
your skin, watering emotions

you thought were comatose
until the rough sea subsides,
creeping out, creeping in.
We are tepid. We are found.

February 13, 2021

Goodfellow

Goodfellow shelters in the forest niche,
seeing by the light of the fireflies,
their golden glow coursing through the trees.
He has far to go, but here he fears the wolves.
They keep to the boundaries, shadowing,
not drawing too near, watching, aloof,
but he sees them, sketches in the dimness.

Sticky roots hold him down, the dirt cleansing,
twilight's leaves comforting his rest.
Here is solitude in broken times.
Ice breaks beyond the forest, flooding out,
its flow creating a severance, the deepest cut.
Pages upon pages; a rock upon the ages.
Life trickles with the falling rain,
light fingers tapping on a hidden path.

February 15, 2023

Orange on white

In the lost winter,
snow flecks blow free in the yard,
lift lightly, skimming.

Carrot-coated fox
creeps, paws trudging twisting lanes,
sniffs the ice-blue air.

Snow slides from branches,
intricate patterns of lace,
the cold pinches all.

Old fox pads lightly,
searches the spiky hedgerows
for dropped morsels.

Bins are easy prey,
these cottages a haven
in the white night.

May 22, 2022

Trance

We seek what we can,
in turning find ourselves in essence,
scraped clean from steamed windows,
the wide-set eyes of the soul.
Squat houses dot the backbone
of this skinny strip, pearl sand sinking out;
chill waters echo the mountain colours
rising like dripping paint on canvas.
A blue arc of tears. Purple sounds.
You can count a hundred breaths here
in the stillness of a pale pink dawn,
this transparent streak of morning
echoing light.

January 15, 2023

Frost

Winter's harshness wanders in,
mist and rain and restless doubt.
Snow courses through the kitchen,
smothering idle clove and cinnamon,
emptying its hands in the corners.
An icy gail blows down quiet corridors
to batter upon the chill windowpanes
where the frost posts its fingerprints.

Even the trees are gathering in,
creeping closer from the forest heart,
uprooting, dragging so many histories
on spiky branches through the hall,
broken twigs walking the twisted staircase
like abandoned breadcrumbs.

The eyes of this house watch the flow
of night, chimney sending up smoke signals
to the new year, emptying itself out,
memories speckling the walls like powder.
Ghosts wander the rooms looking for insight
and someone to whisper their stories to,
but only the trees can hear. Outside, the forest
vibrates with the echo of nature's hum.

January 3, 2023

A round poem

An orange, an apple, a ring
of peel dangling just there.
Without a stair or a style,
simply a curve of the neck,
the loop of a chin, hair curled
on a breeze. A plane's tail
floating in a world of blue.
You can draw a perfect circle
with a protractor, or add
one more to greet infinity.

June 13, 2022

Crossing water (a rondeau)

Listen to the silencing –
they say your journey is a sin.
Our beliefs are who we are, not the things they sow,
they're standing on the high-brow.
Those crossing need a way of being.

They pick numbers that aren't fair,
talk cheaply of life choked of air,
but the people have nowhere to go.
We are listening.

The spin can sound so charming,
but to the victims they're not listening.
Compassion is something we all know,
so surely empathy can only grow?
Who is out there listening?

March 11, 2023

The hotel room

We wander through empty rooms,
stroll lit, indelible silences.
Catch the mood in your eyes,
steal sunlight with your arms.

One table, one chair, one bed.
There's a paucity to the room,
laid out strictly for one person.
Even the rug recoils from two.

The moon moves slowly into orbit,
casting a pallor on the steel balcony
upon which we squeeze ourselves,
ready for the night and its alone

time, the sky a hazy dash of non-
colour. It opens still and cloudless.
We raise our glasses, clink,
taste Prosecco on our tongues

and repaint the day into a Pastoral.
In our imaginations we will fit.
The bed will widen, accommodate
our mutual sleeping patterns.

April 2, 2022

Season's tunes

Sounds of the summer,
laughter in the park, wiles of
dogs barking lively.

Sounds of the springtime,
lemon daffodils through grass,
a half-light of sun.

Sounds of winter spun,
thick crunch of snow, icy sleet,
winds blowing full force.

Sounds of the autumn,
flutter of leaves floating down,
blackbird song on high.

April 24, 2022

This poem was written from a prompt on NaPoWriMo.net.
Prompt: write a poem that anthropomorphises a kind of food. It could be a favourite food of yours or maybe one you feel conflicted about.

Daily bread

I am rising.
I feel myself almost risen,
bubbling below the surface,
indents and permeations.

I smell warm and cosy,
of balmy vanilla and tangy lemon.
My crust will soon have a crispness
that tempts without crumbling,
my middle softly melting,
something to be savoured.

I am rising,
and falling, resting almost.
Tiny currants decorate me,
little eyes looking out.

Hands remove me from the oven,
place me on a metal tray
and I breathe more freely,
happy to escape the sauna
and cool down, the heat bubbles
evanescent from my pores.

April 20, 2022

Out

We're in time,
but the sand has slipped.
It's seeping out, exchanging
glances with the cracked glass.

Out of shape, out of mind,
the material sculpts itself,
becoming something larger,
too big to scoop in one hand.

The radio is a-buzz with words,
a steady multiplication, dishing
out broken fragments on
repeat. We're out of time, exits

blocked with incoming traffic.
All messages are read, except
those that don't echo the
propaganda machine.

A crab scurries quietly, all marks
buried in the sand. Still winds
blow fresh cover, like an ocean ripped.
Those who stood here are voiceless.

September 5, 2022

Silver

We live in huge houses with dead-straight lawns,
grass neatly trimmed around right-angled edges.
See the freshly mowed lines stride out, alternate
light and dark, looking ruled and measured.

Robins and blue tits launch at the iron feeders,
wings a-flutter as they take their lunch to go,
speckling the ground with morsels for squirrels,
while sparrows take a sand bath in the sun dial.

The orange-yolk sun clouds over, clouds off,
and our skin bristles hot and cold in surprise.
Sunglasses put on, sunglasses put down;
we are changeable, like the weather.

Our lapdogs doze by the back door, on food patrol,
smelling of perfume and talc, neatly combed.
Pride of joy is the pink rosebush blooming neatly,
the focal point of our little groomed escape pod.

Our home, more visibly a mansion, stands alone
to attention, every tree pruned, every hedge scalped,
a green sculptured horse a-freeze in mid-gallop.
Seeking adventure, its visa was cancelled.

All the wildness has been sheared or fumed away.
Even the bees have their own section, minute flats
built of wood, manufactured cut-out honeycombs,
while the golden Koi navigate sprouting lily pads.

Windows upon windows upon windows stare out,
too many rooms for one person to clean,
too many rooms to actually live in,
so empty they sit in their pristine perfection.

A sudden newsflash on the iPad flies images
of a drought in a far-flung part of the globe,
and we pause in our reflection of the garden,
reach for our mobile phones, text in a code.

March 25, 2023

This poem was written from a prompt on NaPoWriMo.net.
Prompt: today's prompt is based on Faisal Mohyuddin's poem, 'Five Answers to the Same Question'.
Today, I challenge you to write your own poem that provides five answers to the same question – without ever specifically identifying the question that is being answered. This turned out like a riddle, so the answer is on the back page.

Five answers to the same question (can you guess what it is?)

1.

There was no filter
when we played,
splashing each other
with a snaking hose
all over, cold water
kissing sunburnt skin.

2.

I remember twisting leaves
spilling from the sky.
A resurrection of hope.
Reds, yellows, the burnt
orange an echoed sun.
I gathered them, overflowing
in my upturned palms.

3.

I don't really have a favourite.
I like all four of them. I can't
choose. Each one is different,
showing me something new,
a uniqueness. I look forward
to each one the same.

4.

Daffodils nod in the breeze.
Puffed-up bees bounce between them,
snorkelling in the lemon horns,
vibrating gently inside petals,
little legs poking out,
striped bellies stuck.

5.

We built him in the backyard,
rolled him up from nothing,
stuck round head to torso,
wrapped with a deep, red scarf.
Carrot nose, twiggy arms,
a hat that had seen better days.
We named him Cyril.

April 18, 2022

This poem was written from a prompt on NaPoWriMo.net.
Prompt: write a variation of an acrostic poem. Rather than spelling out a word with the first letters of each line, write a poem that reproduces a phrase with the first words of each line.

Spring awakes with daffodils

So the task is to write an acrostic poem,
paint the ways with ribbons of unique colour
ripped from the heart of a rainbow rising
in a sky dripping with the weight of rain.
Now is the time for a clean rinse of the blue.
Gone are the starlings who through this flew,

arching high, creating intricate patterns
willowing up and down on the ready breeze.
Awakens the night in a few more hours,
key to the opening of night-time's lock.
Ebbing and flowing, the sea takes a turn,
surf leaping and laughing, ever being.

With the moon's light we collect the stars,
inviting them to sup with us tonight,
to take a dip in the deep hazy ocean,
hearts of silver glittering on the wind.

Dancing in the pitch sky, they shimmer so,
an afterthought to dreams of bewitching dust,
forgotten as the hours make their journey
forwards, creeping quick and sinking slow.
Opens the dawn in a blitz of pink and yellow,
decadent in its curtain lift from the blue depths
in which it has slept the dreamscape of the night.
Little do we wonder at these everyday marvels,
so often we have seen them, so seldom gasped in awe.

April 6, 2022

Jackdaw

We've been here before,
said the jackdaw to the rabbit.
This field, this grass, this green,
and all things here come to pass.

You're feeding on the exact same
carrot, munching it in equal fashion,
left to right, up, down, right to left,
and me, wearing my own true feathers
in my dazzling, highfalutin manner,
gazing down at you from up here.

I marvel at your patience, chewing
as if tomorrow depends on it.
But tomorrow is just like today,
and you'll think it's today tomorrow.

June 14, 2022

In the backyard

Blackbird stands stock still, listening
for worms beneath his feet, lemon
beak, bright eye, feathers reflecting
the sun. With a darting head, he digs
swiftly, flicking up dirt for his reward.

The watching cat darts from her hideout,
straight and true, but the blackbird
is faster, spies her, flies like an arrow.
Chastened, the cat ambushes a cricket,
licks her lips, whiskers bristling.

June 12, 2022

The same time

It's the same time that we take
a walk and wonder at the
sparrows in the trees, and
the smells and the wheeze
of spring; its touch and mood,
the way the light glints off,
the however lines of the sun.

A memory skips in and out, and
off we go, recalling small things
we thought we'd long forgot,
resurrected ghosts. It's the
same time as yesterday, same
life, same skin, different colours.

Here we go again, rebeginning
with the fresh meld of spring,
finding hope in an ending,
feeling where a myriad strands
weave, gaining understanding
of how we fit, as we breathe.

June 7, 2022

White light

We light the day,
light the way,
light the way in and out,
count the roots leaving
Earth's cruel soil
to breathe in oxygen
and the salt of the stars.

We greet the night,
nightshade and glade,
night finds its way in and out,
competes with the fireflies
and their neon trails
lighting a faery route
through the sense-blessed green.

We follow the light,
day's breaking might,
night's awe-inspiring foe,
for in the midst of darkness
we will turn to the light,
the purest white, deepest sight,
to wash negativity away.

January 1, 2023

This poem was written from a prompt on NaPoWriMo.net.
Prompt: in the world of well-known poems, maybe there's no gem quite so hoary as Robert Frost's
'The Road not Taken'. I challenge you to write a poem about your own road not taken.

The four-pronged fork

It was a metal fork I picked up,
four-pronged, pointing in its steely way
on this dust-shevelled road.
A gust of rain seemed to choose,
but I was having none of it.

My own footprints veered to the left,
and they say right is always right,
but I chose to go straight ahead,
towards the rain-drenched horizon,
beneath the dripping sky,
sun-bleached and damp-warmed.

The blackbirds charmed me,
a flying long-tailed tit my guide,
and all was quiet on my way,
stepping from one zone to the next,
one time into another,
the past into the future stance.

And we are never ready for the move
until we can think ourselves in it.

The invisible gateway once opened,
what remained behind was left there,
gone now, a misted remembrance,
sealed inside a battered suitcase.

We see circles in the night sky,
of stars and moonlight curves,
and we know we're on our way.

May 3, 2022

This poem was written from a prompt on NaPoWriMo.net.
Prompt: in certain versions of the classic fairytale Sleeping Beauty, various fairies or witches are invited to a princess' christening and bring her gifts. One fairy/witch, however, is not invited and in revenge for the insult lays a curse on the princess. Today, I'd like to challenge you to write a poem in which you muse on the gifts you received at birth.

The bracelet

There was a comet, they said,
crossing the sky on high with colourful
tail feathers, soaring and then disappearing
completely, scattered wide in the pitch.

I have no recollection, being newly born.
I still have a bracelet, so tiny I could never
imagine wearing it again. It's silver and faded,
but it fitted snug on my arm at my christening.

Now it's doll-size. The engraving is hard
to read, but it's still visible. Minute ridges of
a pattern, weaving its way around the band.
It's a small, treasured thing. It's come with me

through my entire life, my silent companion,
living through all the things that make a person.
I lost it recently in a house move. I hunted all over
for this small remembrance of my childhood.

Just a bracelet, but meaning so much more.
A gift from family, a raw bond, a welcoming
into the world, a memory. I wanted to call out,
but never would there come an answer.

If only it could speak. But it is only metal.
Built to last an age.

April 29, 2022

This poem was written from a prompt on NaPoWriMo.net.
Prompt: I'd like to challenge you to write a poem in the style of Kay Ryan, whose poems tend to be short and snappy – with a lot of rhyme and sound play. They also have a deceptive simplicity about them, like proverbs or aphorisms.

With time

With time
we take a trip so shallow,
so deep, so rhythmical,
without pattern or scheme,
something unseen,
down, down, sinking in sand,
treading without knowing
into a trippy sleep
while waking,
not doing anything at all,
without consciousness
of being here,
but wily wishing on stars,
collecting shifting shapes,
a colourful coalescence
of smiles.

April 23, 2022

The circle

Walking into motionless lamp posts,
under ladders, black cats kneading
your heels like dough, seeking to trip –
we run the gauntlet east-to-west
in this incandescent kaleidoscope of hue
ever-revolving, ever-rebecoming
something new, a thing to be known.

You water it, this newborn plant,
skinny strapling reaching for the sun.
But only the moon shines. Agate charm.
It casts a glow where the sun can't reach.

We dispel time, feel it stand still,
shake off our so subtle nuances,
count the creative fingers on each hand,
circle the index three times as if for luck.
Jump puddles, step outside the lines,
avoid endless cracks in paving stones.

And so our rebecoming hasn't come so far
from when we were eight, closing the gate
lest our fathers race out and shout us down,
reminding us not to leave it open.

In this we have come full-circle,
staring into our own eyes, our own selves,
as we were when we were small
and had no idea of what we wanted to be,
or who we might become,
at all.

March 23, 2023

It's time for walkies

I'm pointing to my lead on the back door
because I wanna go for walkies.

I've been taking up your entire bed
for the whole morning long,

but now I want some exercise,
and I think it will do you good.

I wanna go sniff the road
and inspect it for other dogs' doo,

smell the roses and the bushes,
and everything in between too.

Maybe bring the frisbee
so I can show off my prowess,

with a jump and a leap and a twist,
to impress all the lady doggies.

But, hey, we're too late for the school bus.
I won't be able to chase it,

which means I won't pull you flying.
I guess you're relieved about that.

Come on, Bob, the afternoon's young.
We gotta get going. Don't be a lazy human.

I'm a young, strapping Labrador,
and I need my daily exercise,

or I'm gonna chew something up,
and you'll give me your evil glare

that I've dared do something mean
when really I'm your best, best friend.

April 17, 2022

Prisoners of war

It's a waking dream, a split screen,
mirror cracked, no reflective stance.
Figures shadow. Ladders hoisted.
A small scream, a broken nose.
If you cry too loud you might lose
an arm or a leg, or your whole body.

Against this fiery hollowed-out moon,
Macbeth's witches burn a brew on the heath.
Incantations dance like fireflies.
A smokescreen rises from the ashes.
The murdered king is soundless.
The dead can't bear witness.

July 18, 2022

This poem was written from a prompt on NaPoWriMo.net.
Prompt: write a poem about something you have absolutely no interest in. This isn't quite the same, I think,
as something you're indifferent to.

Balls

So your team lost on Thursday night,
and one fell over and cried
after a hard tackle,
and he missed the ball,

and some other guy whipped it
straight into the net instead,
and then another tripped on his laces,
fell splayed across the field,

while the crowd simply groaned,
and someone got red-carded
and another fella got a yellow,
but he wasn't disappointed.

It wasn't his favourite colour,
but it suited him better.
Apparently, the ref was nuts
and needs a new pair of glasses,

and Old Man Whittel's language
needs a good scrubbing out with soap,
but I can't see how a fun time
was had by all.

You're wringing your hands
and swearing at the heavens,
and cursing this team
you'll never watch again...

Until next week.

And you know what?
I don't have a care,
cos I really don't like
this 'beautiful game'.

April 15, 2022

This poem was written from a prompt on NaPoWriMo.net.
Prompt: write a poem that argues against, or somehow questions, a proverb or saying. They say 'all cats are
black at midnight', but really? Surely some of them remain striped. And maybe there is an ill wind that blows
some good.

A bird in the hand

A bird in the hand is worth two
in the bush, so they say,
but some would argue the other way
and seek the bigger prize.

Yet wouldn't you rather a blackbird
sit in the palm of your hand and sing,
its soft feathers fluffing, rustling,
the body shuffling forward for prominence,
almost asking you for a request,
always in tune, always off the cuff,
rhyme and reason matched in song,
these four toes cold to the touch,
obsidian eyes reflecting you.

With chin angled high, notes fly
from staves on a song sheet,
sending a letter into the sky
only you can read.

April 7, 2022

This poem was written from a prompt on NaPoWriMo.net.
Prompt: write a poem in the form of a poetry prompt.

The meadow

1. Wander into a lush, green meadow,
2. breeze through the waving wildflowers
3. and take a moment to learn all their names
4. and indulge their individual fragrances.
5. Count how many drops of dew are shimmering
6. and thread your fingers through the tickly grass.
7. Charge down the hill until your breath explodes
8. and collapse lazily into a blanket of daisies.
9. Pluck only one and count its soft, white petals.
10. The flower head holds the seeds of your poem.

April 4, 2022

Tails

In combination,
the cat and the mouse.
One plays with the other, seeing
safe hands; the other switches
off the safety. Paw on tail,
eyed in two halves, the mouse
can only twitch, its tail caught.

Minutes tick. Time pauses in the way
it does sometimes, the doorway half
ajar between being and not being,
the screen and the van too close,
a stranger's face and eyes appear,
the brakes slam. But that's a story
from age seventeen. The nearly.

The almost. And here we are,
cat and mouse. The mouse is
caught. The mouse knows. The
minutes run endless, seeping into
one long, relentless endurance.
Rain pours. It drips all the way down
the guttering, stealing a course away.

September 8, 2022

Worms

He stands so small,
enclosed within tight fencing

soldier-straight to the sun.
The soil so soft to touch,

he buries his fingers in
deep, searching for movement.

In sienna shorts, long socks
and sandals, his golden locks

dazzle, blue eyes fixed on his task.
His pawing soon finds one. Tensing,

he surrounds it, digs it out.
It squirms, the pink flesh peeking

through his fist at the day,
seeking the safety of lost soil.

The boy laughs and runs inside,
grasping his trophy of the earth.

April 2, 2022

Lost & Found

At the Lost & Found,
they look into brown puppy-dog eyes,
stare in deep, see a furry face light up,
tongue roll, watch the whip-tail wag
the backside off, find themselves in another being –
one they can take care of, like a child.

A pup they can take for a meandering walk
in the park, play with, who will maybe guard them;
a creature that takes away the loneliness
of an empty day and gives back what they're given.

When anyone exits a bell clangs above the door.
To the shop owner, it's just another sale.
But the visitors leave with a jaunt in their step,
blissfully unaware that they're really the ones
who have just been found.

May 17, 2023

Gold

Alice says she knows your brother,
Alice says she knows Everyman.
Once, the streets were paved with gold,
but now we wade through mustard.
There is a power play they hold up high,
the ministry of something chilly,
and down here the bells have yet to toll,
to reveal what we already know.

It takes a while to take a picture.
You've got to get the focus right,
the angle, disintegrate the blur,
no shake; the snake, a second skin,
the in-between of the invisible view.
Here we go again, seeing it anew,
the past, the future, present tense,
just redrawn, resketched, tangible.

April 8, 2023

Superstition

We walk in superstition,
black cats criss-crossing our path,
dodging ladders sliding from windows
and leaping over pavement fissures,
seeking to avoid any imaginary pitfall
to press snooze on destiny.

We lock the metal gate behind us,
seal the windows, close the shades,
turn the welcome mat the other way,
and cross ourselves lest we see him
lurking in the shadows of the scenes,
dragging his scythe through the dirt.

February 25, 2023

Hourglass

Time and, again,
time. It seeps through the
cracks, the edges, pursuing
future, past and present,
casting waves in sand,
a leaking of sensation,
collecting, gathering days,
seconds and circumstance,
a measure of the hour,
as the glass turns,
minutes being just moments
of a life travelling to
the end.

August 15, 2022

This poem was written from a prompt on NaPoWriMo.net.
Prompt: name your alter ego, and then describe him/her in detail. Then write in your alter ego's voice.

The alter ego (gecko)

Lygodactylus williamsi of the Gekkonidae family
is critically endangered out here in the wild.
The gecko's electric-blue, black-striped sheen
attracts too many collectors who take them home
to enclose them in leafy terrariums under heat lamps,
a poor substitute for the glorious Tanzanian sunshine
and a playground of towering Pandanus palm trees.

These lizards span 31 inches from nose to tail tip,
with a surprisingly orange underbelly hidden away.
Adhesive toe pads mean they can stick to and climb up
just about anything, even glass. They're easy-going,
but backed into a corner they will hiss at any would-be assassin.
Every few weeks they shed their skin in a slow striptease,
gobbling up their costume by the end of the day.

***

"I like to bask in the sun, daylight being my favourite time,
for at night you'll catch me napping. I like the misted air of dawn,
catching dew on my tongue to drink, rustling through the leaf litter
on the ground as I creep my way through the forest floor.

We know the Collectors by sight and I'm fast to steal myself away,
out of fear of being caught and never seeing my home again.
No one has ever returned to tell the tale of where they've been.
I wonder if it's another forest or somewhere completely alien.

Some people call us the turquoise dwarf or William's dwarf gecko,
but mainly we're known as the electric blue, although we females
of the species are sometimes green. Unusually, I'm a bright cyan.
I live in the Kimboza Forest snug in the foothills of the Uluguru Mountains.

My home is the *Pandanus rabaiensis* screwpine tree, and I'm fondest
of the leaf crown. My dinner is made up of small leaf insects and nectar
is my equivalent of a chocolate treat. My best friend, Amon, is brighter
than me, a brilliant blue with the power to dazzle you in the sunshine.

He is a gecko of many moods, prone to head-bobbing, tail-wagging
and even throat-puffing. I can never tell which way he's going to go.
Our first batch of eggs was laid a week ago, two in total, and I'm excited
for them to hatch. It should take 60 to 90 days. Tell you a secret, I can't wait."

April 8, 2022

Thank you for buying this book. I hope you enjoyed it.
Please leave a review – feedback is always welcome.

The answer to the poem 'Five answers to the same question' is: which season do you like best?

About the author

Vickie Johnstone lives in London, writing stories, songs and poetry.
Some day she hopes to live by the sea with fluffy cats and a lifetime supply of
Milky Bar chocolate.

For a free copy of an ebook of mine of your choice,
just contact me on Facebook or twitter.
Cheers, Vickie.

Have a gorgeous day. I hope the sun is shining!

Blog: www.vickiejohnstone.blogspot.com

Twitter: @vickiejohnstone

Facebook author page: www.facebook.com/AuthorVickieJohnstone

www.ingramcontent.com/pod-product-compliance
Lightning Source LLC
Chambersburg PA
CBHW060610120726
48002CB00010B/2907